7 Steps To Be A Killer Mentor

A Starter's Guide to Helping
Others Achieve Their Dreams

By Austin Pritchard

Table of Contents

Introduction	4
1. Be Available	7
2. Be Empathetic	6
3. Be Vulnerable	9
4. Be In Tune	13
5. Be Inquisitive	17
6. Be Present	20
7. Be Focused	25
About the Author	26

This book is dedicated to all the mentors
who have helped be become the man I am today.
Thank you to each person who chooses to
invest time and wisdom into others.

INTRODUCTION

You have probably found yourself reading this book through my blog. Maybe a friend referred you to this resource. Whatever your journey here, I'm glad you've arrived.

Welcome to 7 Steps To Be A Killer Mentor.

Mentors made me better.

It is from this personal testimony of the power found in a mentor relationship that I have worked to write this book. The main purpose of this book is to help empower you as a mentor. Our families, communities, and world become better one relationship at a time.

I look back across each stage of my life and identify key people who took the time to live out these seven mentoring elements before me.

Mentoring is a process.

Mentoring is a skill you only develop through practice. I know you have the heart to make a difference with people. That's why you are reading this book.

To everyone who is reading this book, I am so blessed by your support. I hope this book helps empower you to begin making a difference in the lives of those you engage. This is the start of something special in your life and in the life of each person that sits across from you.

BE AVAILABLE

MAKE IT PUBLIC

People are looking for mentors. It is important to openly communicate that you desire to help by being a mentor. As you consider becoming a mentor, think about how you will let people know you want to be a mentor.

There are organizations that help to foster the initial connection between mentor and mentee, like the Boy & Girls Club and Mentoring.org, that work to partner mentors with youth. These types of organizations are great if you are looking to work with youth.

Let's focus on mentoring at the adult level. There are agencies that help to match individuals seeking to mentor fellow adults. A great place to start is with your local community services (YWCA, Community Centers, Churches, Advocacy Centers).

But let's make it even more granular. Since you are reading this book I'm going to make an assumption. There are already people in your life that you have thought about mentoring.

You have a circle of influence.

It is within this is circle that you will see a regular need for mentoring.

SCHEDULE TIME

We communicate something very specific through our schedules. We make time for what we value. When you set aside time in your schedule you convey, at the very beginning, how important the mentee is to you.

Where will you fit time with the people you are mentoring?

As you consider what being a mentor means, think about the specifics of adding a new relationship to your life. How will you meet? Where will you meet? When will you meet?

By identifying key locations to meet and blocking out specific times of availability you set the tone for the whole relationship.

CLARITY IS KING

Don't be ambiguous with your time. It's important to be available and let people know that you want to mentor them - convey your interest and desire.

The worst thing you can do is leave a mentor relationship open for anything. This fosters no commitment in the process.

The best thing you can do is create parameters for the relationship to develop. If you're able to offer a morning or two, in the week, one evening a week, or an hour on the weekend, you begin to create a context where options exist. You are also creating this structure to help filter your mentees. Requiring mentees to adjust their schedule is an effective means to measure early commitment.

This will help weed out people who think they want to be mentored but don't have the drive to follow through.

REMEMBER

Your time is valuable.

While you desire to help the people striving to make it through life; you can only help someone who first wants to be helped.

You will avoid much frustration by setting clear parameters for your mentoring relationships.

BE EMPATHETIC

Empathy is not problem-solving.

WANT TO HELP

You are not trying to solve problems. You are trying to connect emotionally with what people are trying to achieve. When you build empathy toward someone, you build a connection. You begin to understand why they care about what they want to do.

If you approach mentoring as a problem to solve you miss the greatest opportunity for effective change.

Your goal is to cultivate a skill-set within a person. When this happens, the mentee begins problem-solving on their own. Don't just give solutions to problems teach critical teaching skills, while creating an independent problem-solver. The greatest gift a mentor can give is the possibility to view things from a new perspective. Over time your mentee will begin to find solutions where they only saw problems before.

Remember: Empathy works to understand another person's situation from their perspective. You are fighting the cultural trend of individualism by connecting person to person. (Read more about empathy at www.psychologytoday.com)

DEVELOP OVER RESCUE

It is very important to not confuse sympathy with empathy.

When you are sympathetic toward someone there is a level of separation between you – a disconnect of emotion. Sympathy takes a position of "I am h
ere and you are there; boy I feel sorry for you."

When you empathize, you work to relate and understand what a person feels. You connect.

Empathy relates you to your mentee's situation. You care because it's important. Find a connection to your life, draw on how you felt in a similar situation.

As you work to build empathy for with your mentee, it is important not to be led by your emotions. As a mentor, people are coming to you for guidance. They are already emotional over what they are doing (or trying to do).

Your mentee needs you to relate to their struggle and then help bring clear, logical focus to their goal. They don't need another friend to validate their emotions.

Mentors don't parrot emotion; they channel it.

Sympathy quickly leads to pity. Out of pity you will try to fix a problem and alleviate the distress your mentee is feeling. This truly, deeply, speaks to the quality of who you are as a person; but is not helpful for a mentor. After you are done with your time together, you and your mentee will feel "deeply connected" and have nothing resolved.

Empathy equals you caring enough about what your mentee is dealing with to not react emotionally or try to take over and solve the problem.

Sympathetic rescuers become overwhelmed and ineffective providers of direction.

The most caring and empathetic thing you can do for a person is work with them. Your goal is to develop skills in a mentee that produce solutions.

Strive to build problem solvers over solving other's problems.

BE VULNERABLE

People want a human. No one goes to superman for advice.

SHARE SUCCESS

You have achieved something in life and people want to know about it.

Go ahead and brag a little bit, that's why the person sitting across the table agreed to be there. If you have a story that will help inspire your mentee, don't hold it back.

People want to know they can win. Your mentee is hoping you are living, breathing proof they can achieve their goal.

Success is contagious. As you share your success, it builds vision in the hearts and minds of the people who are listening to you. You are the proof that a dream or idea can become a tangible reality.

People feel that when they talk about themselves and their accomplishments they are being selfish and self-centered. This is true of some individuals. Most people hold back what they have to offer out of fear - fear of being perceived as self-centered, fear of coming across as better than others, fear of being rejected.

These are real fears, but these fears are the roadblocks that hold your mentor experience from having deep success.

Sharing success builds hope.

SHARE FAILURE

Be authentic. No one gets it right 100% of the time.

It's hard to talk about when you win: it's tougher to share your failures. Those times you stepped out to bring a dream from imagination land into reality-only to see that beautiful unicorn murdered by the dull, jagged blade of failure.

Inconceivable.

I love this word, inconceivable. It reminds me of my wife's favorite movie, *The Princess Bride*.

One of the antagonists continually uses the statement: "Inconceivable!" He is trying to express the improbability of different events unfolding. All are unlikely. None are inconceivable.

(Seriously, if you haven't seen *The Princess Bride* or it's been more than a month, stop reading this book and watch it, your laugh meter will thank you.)

How many times have you looked at your past and seen failure? How many sad, heart wrenching, unicorn deaths have you mourned? It's difficult to see the silver lining that follows failure.

But you have learned what only failure teaches. The maturity you possess is invaluable to those you invest into.

Don't allow the pain of your failures to create an inconceivable narrative for success. Far too often the thought of recovering from a failure is inconceivable. That fear is paralyzing. Your story can liberate your mentee from the crippling grip of the fear of failure. Reframe your story. Use your failures as the foundation for future success.

Let no unicorn die in vain. Share the story of each unicorn past. Let the lessons of their life live in every mentee's avoidance of their miss-steps.

Wins and losses. That's every situations outcome. We all strive to win at whatever we do. You are reading this book because you want to win at mentoring. You want to help those around you. The difficult truth is that you won't succeed 100% of the time.

There will be mentee relationships that just don't work out. It could be personality conflicts. Though, if handled with tact, differences can be a great asset to a mentor relationship. Sometimes beliefs and methodology won't align, and the relationship will just dissolve. Other times you will pour time and energy into a person only to have it repaid with combativeness.

Don't let the unsuccessful relationships discourage you from continuing to work as a mentor. For every letdown there will be moments where someone finally "gets it" and you witness true breakthrough in their life.

SHARE VALIDATION

Help normalize the situation.

It is easy to look at the struggle we go through and think that it is unique to us. Your mentee will have struggles, relationships, and conflicts that feel embarrassing and overwhelming.

Insurmountable situations are simply problems we have yet to find the answer for.

When you are able to normalize, never minimize, your mentee's struggle, you allow for there to be light at the end of the tunnel.

Allowing for emotion is critical to validation. Consider the appropriate emotion for the situation and then evaluate what a healthy response would be to the emotion and situation. Empower your mentee to explore his or her emotions and give them names. There are many resources like emotions wheels and charts to help give name to your mentee's emotions.

Role-play is a great tool for a mentor to bring to the table. If your mentee is angry over a situation and wants to throat punch someone, play it out - verbally. Begin to ask open-ended questions: How would you feel if you punched that person? What would happen if you hurt your hand? Could you afford to miss work? What problem does this solve? Could that choice create more problems? What would be some alternatives to the lethal throat punch?

The key is to allow for the mentee to come to their own decision without you giving solutions. We want to promote self-actualization in our mentees.

Channel your best Socrates.

BE IN TUNE

A good mentor is like an old friend, they just get you.

LISTEN WELL

One little factor can instantly connect you to another person. Listen more than you talk. But it's about more than not speaking. To connect with a person, you have to care about what they are going through.

Creating space for someone to talk is good. Understanding why they need to talk is better.

In a counseling session, the recommended talking to listening ratio is 5:1. So, in an hour counseling session, a competent counselor will only talk about 10 minutes.

Next time you are in a group, try to focus on observing over responding. See how much you can learn about the topic being discussed and the people participating in the discussion.

Great mentors are great observers.

With your mentee, listen to understand. Provide the space for them to process what they are working on verbally. We gain insight into what we are going through as we talk about it.

SILENCE

Any space of time where two or more people are silent for 5 seconds or more – is silence. Try taking deliberate pauses in conversations. This allows your mentee time to process all that is being discussed. There is nothing more powerful in a relationship than silence. It communicates more than any words can. You've probably encountered the negative effects of silence: stonewalling, avoidance, the looming cold-shoulder. Silence is often used in moments where people want to avoid a conflict, but instead conflict is prolonged.

Silence is hard. Have you ever attempted to not speak on purpose? I often sit in meetings and just listen and observe what is happening. The person driving the meeting has an agenda they want to accomplish, often collaboration around a thought topic.

In order to get feedback, ask a question. In order to get good feedback, ask good questions then wait. A posed question craves an answer.

When you ask a question, you want an answer. Yet, those receiving your questions are at a disadvantage. They aren't in your mind. It's quite possible that when they hear your question it's the first time they have mentally chewed on it.

Let the question steep for a moment. It always feels longer and more awkward for you than for those who are processing your question.

Think tea not instant coffee. Tea takes time to steep. The water must draw out the dehydrated goodness hidden in the dried tealeaves. Your question is a tea bag. Those you ask questions to are the hot water that draws out the hidden treasures of your brilliant, well-crafted question.

We like fast, and speed often wins over quality; hence, the survival of instant coffee. It takes no time for instant brew coffee to reach its full potential. Even regular brewed coffee is fast. That's why Keurig works. That's why you can pull the pot off the burner and pour coffee right into your mug before it's done brewing. What's there, in the carafe, is ready for consumption.

Don't take silence or a delayed response as a negative response. Reframe your mentee's delay as a deliberate processing of deep thought and meaning. Allow the space to respond.

This is going to suck. Your mind is going to race in 100 different directions. You will want to clarify. You will want to give more details. You will want to prompt an answer. You will want to run away and cry because you feel like you completely missed connecting with the person sitting across from you.

But wait, invoke deliberate patience and allow for your mentee to steep on the question.

Then, just when you think you are going to literally die, they will say something. If your mentee needs more clarification, guess what, they will. Remember, mentor relationships are cups of tea not mugs of coffee.

THINK POSTURE

How you present yourself plays a big part in how you are received. Make conscious effort to sit squarely to your mentee. Have an open posture; think shoulders back, chin up, and never cross those arms. Your eye contact matters. When you make deliberate eye contact, you instantly communicate your commitment to the person you're looking at. Relax your body and face. If you look uncomfortable your mentee will feel uncomfortable. Use friendly expressions.

Your nonverbals communicate more than you ever say, before you ever say it.

(BONUS) PERSONAL SPACE

Sit about 5 feet apart. Think about the cultural context of your mentee. What is their comfort level of personal space? If you sit too far away you communicate disinterest, plus it's just hard to hear and talk at a distance. The nuisances of nonverbals are lost over distance. Consider text messages. Have you ever been misunderstood? Or how about receiving a text IN ALL CAPS? Seriously, stop yelling at me.

Too much space creates ambiguity, too little space creates discomfort.

MENTOR ALLIANCE

The mentor alliance defines the strength of your relationship. The stronger the alliance, the greater the outcome will be along the mentoring journey.

The mentor alliance is simply the degree a mentee trusts and opens up to their mentor. Collaboration and empathy are the two key components in every mentor alliance. Every person wants to be an active part of their process and they want to know you care specifically about them.

Your alliance begins at the first exchange and directly reflects how comfortable your mentee is?

Active listening is an amazing tool that builds pocket-change in a new relationship. It also helps strengthen and reinforce existing relationships.

The key to active listening is to listen to understand versus waiting to respond. Did you know that on average we speak at about 125 words per minute? Do you know how many words you can mentally process in a minute? The answer is roughly 400!

That means you are only using 1/3 of your mental capacity while listening to someone. What are you doing with the other 2/3s of your mental capacity?

I'm normally drafting my opinion, rebuttal, and advice while listening to someone. Which leads to my wife's least favorite trait of mine – interrupting. When I begin to pre-compose my response before establishing clear understanding of what is being said, I'm only concerned with my part of the conversation. I miss the opportunity to understand what my wife is saying. I miss the moment of making her feel valued.

When you listen only to acquire the information you need to insert your response, you will miss the opportunity to truly and deeply understand your mentee. You miss the fleeting moment of instilling value.

Mentors should work to understand meaning, feeling, and intention. Only when there is a full understanding of what a person means, how they feel about the topic, and why they care, can we process a valuable contribution to the conversation.

BE INQUISITIVE

The key to being inquisitive without just being noisy is asking good questions.

ASK GOOD QUESTIONS

Don't simply seek information. You must be self-aware as a mentor and avoid the temptation to be caught up in the life-story of your mentee. The temptation is to become a conversational-voyeurist.

WHAT MATTERS MORE

It's important to identify what you are going to do. It's more important to identify what the person you are mentoring is going to do. A person's "what" is more important than their "why". We'll talk about why in just a second. I want to close out this section by talking about "why". Why is very important, however we are often confused as to which "why" we should talk about.

When you know what you're going to do, you've allowed yourself to define when and how. If you don't know what you're going to do, you just go blasting a shotgun in the dark and pick-up whatever falls to the ground. It's not productive to live with a philosophy of throwing darts in the dark and seeing what you hit.

WHEN IS KEY

Just like when you became specific about your availability to mentor, your mentee needs to be specific about their goals.

If you want to do something, but never assign a time, it will never get done. Say you want to write a book, but never say when you'll start, you may not start. You have no motivation or accountability to complete that goal. You may start it and dabble in it, but it won't get completed. There will always be something else that comes up and overtakes the desire you have to write a book until it's made a clear priority.

Mentors do more than talk about dreams, they accomplish them. Your mentee won't hang around long if all you have to offer is talk about ideas. You must bring lessons learned from action into the conversation.

HOW IS SUBJECTIVE

We all have opinions on how to do, well, everything.

One of my favorite stories is from when I was a teenager. One of my chores was to rake leaves. Now, there are multiple ways to rake leaves, but my dad had a very specific way he thought it should be done. I had a way I thought it should be done. And the reality was that these two opinions didn't match perfectly. There were differences.

Now we could talk about the lessons we can learn from the differences between how people do a task; but as a mentor, it is important to realize that your way of accomplishing something is not the only way to do something.

Often, we get locked into one way of doing something because it worked before. Therefore, we think that is the only right way to get the job done. The reality is, when raking leaves, as long as the leaves are gone, the job is accomplished.

There is the element of coaching and advice giving that you get to do during the how phase. These are best practices and recommendations over exact instructions on how to accomplish a goal.

If you approach the input stage of a mentor relationship from a position of providing options for your mentee to choose from, you empower your mentee through decision-making. Share what worked well for you. Include other approaches you've seen work well. You don't have to shy away from mistakes either. Share what hasn't worked as well and consider what you might have done different in those times of failure.

You want to give feedback: there are ways to be more effective and speed up the process. Mentees are literally seeking advice to achieve a better result.

The rub is you don't want your mentee to feel like they are losing their identity or have to become a clone of you to be successful in their endeavors.

What your mentee is trying to accomplish should always match who they are. Your mindset as a mentor is to find and hold onto the identity of the mentee.

WHY IS MISLEADING

There are two "why's" in life. Why things happen and why you act. Why things happen can't always be answered. Why you act can be determined.

When considering why you do something, the question that needs to be asked is, "what changes if I find out why?" When we think we need to know why something happens, you lose sight of what you are doing and how you are going to do it.

An example of a good why is: "why am I going to go back to school?" Knowing why you want to go to school will help you conquer the hard times.

Knowing "why" is always second to "what".

When I don't have the energy or the drive, when it's no longer fun, why dies. Unless your "why" connected to "what" is being accomplished, time and challenges will always defeat even the clearest of "whys".

A "why" alone always dies when fun ends.

When you know what you are going to do you are more likely to finish when it gets hard.

BE PRESENT

People want your complete attention. There is nothing worse than feeling like you are second to someone or something else.

FULLY ENGAGED

As I engage in more meetings and counseling sessions, I notice something - distractions.

We all have distractions. In our current culture, it's almost impossible to disconnect from what is happening around you. Phones connect us continuously to the world at large and our friends and family – instantly.

Think about a scenario where you expected someone's complete attention. Maybe you even paid for it. The doctor is a great example. Before you go in for a visit, you schedule an appointment. There is a set time for you to meet. You arrive and sit in a waiting room for your doctor to become available. Eventually, you are escorted back to a room set just for you. You wait, awkwardly, alone, wondering what is in the cupboard and how much trouble you would get into if you started to play doctor.

Then the knock - your doctor enters the room.

It may only be for five-minutes, but during that time you command the doctor's full attention.

Now, what if the doctor had just come to the initial waiting room and asked the group of patients waiting to be seen, "What brings you in today?"

Whether it's two people or fifteen people, there is an expectation that isn't being met. When the doctor engages multiple people at once he is fully engaged with no one.

Your expectation of having the doctor's complete attention and mind-space is valid.

In the same way, your mentee's expectation of having you be fully engaged with them is valid. You must be able to be engaged with your mentee exclusively during your scheduled time. This means mentally as well as physically.

Where you meet is important. You are creating an environment that fosters trust and openness. But, environment is second to your mentee's need for you to have clear mind-space. The list of everything else you have to do beyond your mentor time must be stored away.

When your focus is elsewhere, people notice; you are under performing.

Think about your mind-space like an internet browser window. The more tabs you have open the harder it is to keep track of everything. When there is just one tab open, you are completely focused on that material. When there are thirteen tabs open, your thoughts are spread thin, bouncing from tab to tab, topic to topic. Furthermore, when you have too many things running through your brain, you process information slower. Just as a computer slows down when too many programs are running at once, you will be engaged at a lower effectiveness if you have other matters competing for your mind-space.

As you open more mental tabs, you begin to miss the live stream of information that is happening in front of you.

Effective mentoring happens in the midst of battling mental drift. Keeping on task is difficult. Think about how easy it is to get distracted as you read this book. Your effectiveness as a mentor will be directly connected to how well you can refocus when you begin to drift.

SILENCE DISTRACTIONS

Has this ever happened to you? You are talking to someone about what's happening in your life and his or her phone goes off? Just like that, in a single moment, the momentum of your conversation halts.

In a mentor relationship, there is a greater affect - trust is broken. I've been on a job interview and during the interview the employer's phone kept chiming. At one point, the interview actually stopped so she could check and answer her phone. Honestly, that experience made me question whether I wanted to continue pursuing employment there.

You may feel that you can't disconnect. What if something happens and people need to reach you?

The truth is, if there is an emergency, you can be reached. There are coworkers, office administrators, and even police who can reach you. You'd be surprised how fast and easily you can be reached, even when you try to disconnect.

The harder part is to allow yourself to be released from expectations. There are two expectations you must overcome, those you place on yourself and those others place on you. You will battle the temptation of elevating important items to emergency items.

As you work to create an open environment of trust and freedom to share don't let external elements derail you progress.

Turn off televisions, silence radios, and limit external human interactions.

Mentoring is hard work; don't make your journey harder by allowing controllable elements to run unchecked.

Even writing this book I'm on my laptop that is connected to the internet and all my different accounts. Emails, text messages, social media, and more are screaming for my attention. Sometimes I forget to turn off the notifications on my laptop and put my phone on silent (and place it screen down) when I start writing. And guess what? As soon as I start to get into a flow, hashing out a thought, DING, a notification.

BE FOCUSED

Focus depicts a clear vision.

A vision for a specific outcome produces results. You execute that vision by maintaining a clear picture of "who, what, when, why, and where" then you will have a productive mentor relationship. Keep in focus who is being mentored. Hold what you want to accomplish ever in front of you. Stick to the when (time and length) of the relationship. Be clear about why you want to be a mentor. Be consistent in your approach to where mentoring happens. Maintain your focus of how you will mentor.

GOALS, DESIRES, DREAMS

It's easy to see potential in others. You may express your keen eye of observation through statements like, "Man, they are so talented" or "If I had their talent I would …" The truth is, it's easier to critique someone else.

Mentors must be cautious to not live vicariously. Mentoring is not about achieving the things we would do if we were someone else. Mentoring is simply empowering someone to achieve their dream.

The focus of a mentor is always outwardly focused; considering what the mentee is working toward and then aiding them to reach their goal.

Think about providing perspective and giving input through questions over giving advice through statements.

Great mentees have their own goals. Hopefully, they have even completed a few. Mentors have dreams for their life, independent of mentee dreams. Your purpose as a mentor must be focused on your mentee's dreams.

There is an old proverb that essentially says, wise people love searching out meaning; it's an honor to help others find meaning in their lives.

People look for a mentor to accomplish a specific goal. Seldom will a person seek help in a broader, help me figure out my whole life, context. Mentors have the honor to help identify mentees' dreams and bring focus to their desires.

CONCLUSION

Mentors are extremely valuable. I would bet you had someone in your mind that impacted your life as you read this book.

It's because of the people, like you, who make it a priority to exemplifying these seven traits in their life that people are able to get unstuck and accomplish amazing dreams. Those who have the passion to help others reach their dreams are invaluable. As you begin new mentor relationships and work to improve existing relationships, I hope these seven traits help you become a better mentor. May you continue to foster the development of many and see every unicorn you dream of grow to a reality.

Remember great mentors are:
Available
Empathetic
Vulnerable
Listeners
Inquisitive
Present
Focused

When you enter a relationship with the goal to understand and help, you create the environment to accomplish amazing things.

Thank you for taking the time to read this book.

ABOUT THE AUTHOR

Austin is a pastor and soon to be therapist in the south-central Pennsylvania area. He has a passion for helping people reach their fullest potential and achieve their dreams.

He spent 12-years in the U.S. Air Force where he focused on leading teams, providing support to deployed team members, and overseeing tactical training.

Austin received his Associates Degree in Electronics from the University of the Air Force. In 2016, he earned a Bachelor of Science in Interdisciplinary Studies from Liberty University and will receive his Master of Arts in Marriage and Family Therapy from Liberty University the spring of 2019. He recently begun interning with a local counseling agency.

Being a husband and father is one of Austin's greatest joys. Austin lives in Pennsylvania with Teresa his wife and two daughters, Aurora and Damaris.

You can read more about Austin at
www.austinnpritchard.com/about

You can also listen to his podcast on relationships at
www.austinnpritchard.com/podcast

You can find and connect with Austin on social media at:
Facebook: austinnpritchard
Instagram: austinnpritchard
Twitter: pritchard_an

www.ingramcontent.com/pod-product-compliance
Lightning Source LLC
Chambersburg PA
CBHW030602220526
45463CB00007B/3149